The Digital Nomad Lifestyle

Making a Living Online

From Your RV

Janet Smith

Introduction... 5

Reality Checks... 7

OK, let's get started with the online business!... 11

SEO (Search Engine Optimization)... 23

Social Media Marketing... 27

Staying Connected Online... 31

Offline Ways to Make Money... 33

What Type of RV is Right for YOU?... 39

Determining Your Lifestyle and Comfort Levels... 49

Where to Park It?... 53

The RV Electrical System... 61

Introduction

I have been living and working online, fulltime in a motorhome, for 3 years as of this writing, May 2016. I'm not making a fortune, but certainly making enough to maintain this lifestyle. I make a living with self publishing, paperbacks, Kindle, iBook and MP3s, affiliate marketing, You Tube, Android apps, Google AdWords and AdMob, Etsy, travel photography, and any other angle I can find.

I have been traveling in the Southwestern states, part time "boondocking", part time in RV parks, and part time in Walmart and Indian casino parking lots. I'll share with you what I know about making money online, about mobile internet, and "boondocking", RVer terminology for living off grid.

This won't happen overnight, and I suggest you get started now, while you're still living in "sticks and bricks". Start building your income online, and also, thoroughly research the RV lifestyle. Arm yourself with plenty of knowledge before you hit the road. I hope this booklet provides you with some ideas, and a starting point for your journey!

Reality Checks

I have an active You Tube channel (one source of income) and some of the comments I get, and other RVers on You Tube get, gives me clues as to the "common misperceptions" many have about mobile internet and the RV lifestyle.

#1: "Why do you waste money on Verizon? You could get Sprint/T-Mobile unlimited, for a lot cheaper!"

Answer: I want you to look at these cell coverage comparison maps, and compare the coverage outside of the major metro areas: http://www.cellularmaps.com/net_compare.shtml If you have not spent a lot of time outside of the big cities, you may not be aware that in many rural areas, there is no cell coverage at all, especially if you don't have Verizon, and especially in the Western states. If you plan to stay in the big cities, then any plan might do, but if you plan on boondocking, or traveling in the national parks and scenic rural areas, then it's Verizon, or maybe AT&T. And don't under estimate how many GBs you'll need; 15-30 GBs per month, depending on useage should do it. If your business plan includes uploading a lot of videos, images, apps or other media, don't skimp. Verizon charges $10 per extra GB, so if you run short before the end of the month, it could cost you big.

#2: "Why do you waste money at all on a data plan? Why don't you just use the free wifi at McDonalds, Starbucks, or the RV park?"

Answer: In many small towns and rural places, there are

no McDonalds, Starbucks, or any other place that provides free wifi. Besides, how long can you reasonably sit around in a McDonalds or Starbucks? I once spent 1 ½ hours in a McDonald's, uploading one 8 minute video, and it wasn't even full HD. Contrary to popular belief, it takes longer than an hour a day to make money online, at least at first. RV park wifi is usually pretty poor, with slow speeds. Also, many RV parks use a service called TengoNet, which throttles your use, so no streaming videos, super slow uploads and downloads, and, they will cut you off, once the system senses you are doing more than simply checking email or reading the news. Of course, if it's available to you, take advantage of free wifi, but I would not count on it, not if you want to make money online.

#3: "Why do you use old fashioned GPS and paper maps? Why don't you just get a smart phone, and use apps?"

Answer: Because a smart phone is not going to work in areas without decent 3G or 4G coverage, and also, you can burn up a lot of GBs streaming data, especially on a long trip. Also, if you look at a paper map, you can get an overview of an area, and you'll see places on the map you might not otherwise discover, like rest stops, wilderness areas and the lesser known state and national parks. You can also make notes on a paper map, for future reference.

#4: "Why aren't you driving cross country, constantly moving, *seeing and doing everything*? Why aren't you driving to Alaska, or going Back East? Don't you want to see *everything and every place*?"

Answer: Driving a motorhome, or a big truck pulling a trailer, costs a lot in gas money! Wear and tear repairs also cost. Driving a motorhome or towing a trailer can also be a lot more challenging and tiring than driving a car. Parking for a few weeks or months at a time, can be economical, and less stressful, than moving and driving every few days.

The monthly rates at RV park are generally a lot cheaper than the daily or weekly rates, and as for boondocking, you want to stay west of the Rockies for abundant BLM land, and aim for the places where you can stay for two weeks or more. The less frequented and less touristy areas are also less expensive, and easier to get into. Also, if you find someplace with good free wifi, or excellent 4G, why not stay awhile, and appreciate the scenery! *One tip for small town rural RV parks; bring cash or paper checks, many won't take debit or credit cards.*

Some Misconceptions About an Online Business

#1: I can sit on the beach or the deck of a sail boat, and make millions.

Answer: You're probably not going to get 3G or 4G at the beach, and you won't be able to see your screen in the sun anyways. And if you're trying to do it all yourself, from the beach or a boat, you're not making millions. If you were, you'd have an assistant.

#2: I can find that *one thing*, and make a fortune!

Answer: Making money online is generally a nickel and dime affair, a little here, a little there. Even if you choose *one thing* to promote, you'll need to promote it through a variety of social media, like Facebook, Twitter, Pinterest, Instagram, You Tube, and all the others, which means, you'll need to learn about each, and spend time on each. (Using a service like Buffer.com or Hootsuit.com can make that easy, more on that later). You may also need to promote through one or more of your own websites, which means you'll need to learn the basics of webmastering and SEO (search engine optimization). You may also choose to promote through advertising on other people's websites, or PPC (pay per click) advertising, so you'll need to learn about that. Making a living with *one thing*, promoted through *one thing*, isn't likely to earn you a living.

#3: I can work just four hours a day, or four hours a week, and make a 6-figure income!

Answer: At least at the beginning, you are going to have to work a *lot* more than four hours a day, or four hours a week. It may take years to get things set up to the point where your business is running on autopilot. And even if you do get it running on auto, the web is constantly changing, the economy keeps getting more expensive, and you'll need to constantly be tweaking, upgrading and updating, to stay on top.

OK, let's get started with the online business!

First thing you need to figure out is, your niche market. It could be almost anything, but preferably something you are knowledgeable about, have a passion for, and that other people are interested in. It could be a craft skill you have, music, art, it could be consulting or counseling skills, computer programming, website skills, or marketing skills. Basically, it will break down to selling products and services; yours, other people's, and a combination of both.

What are the three key things to consider when pursuing a niche market?

Find ways to meet the unique needs of your potential buyers. What is important to them, what can improve their lives, and improve the way they do things? As an example, let's say you have experience as a dog trainer; writing books and creating online training seminars that are breed specific would be a niche. A Pitbull will have different training requirements than, let's say, a Bloodhound. Using this as an example, you would join some breed specific online forums, to find out what was important to those particular breed pet-parents. In addition to your own knowledge, you would study what other expert dog trainers had to say about each breed type. Then you would write your books, and create your websites, using that breed specific knowledge.

Learn to speak the language of your niche market. There

are certain key words and phrases unique to each market, as well as different emotional needs and expectations. Using the dog training example again, the Pitbull owner has a different reason for choosing that breed than the Bloodhound owner, and each has a unique language when discussing their breed. In order to convey your expertise, and your products, it's vital to learn the lingo.

Do some test marketing. You can do this by investigating your competition online. You can search Amazon, and other online markets, and take a look at the popularity of titles related to your subject. How are they selling? *(Or not selling?)* Study the keywords they are using, the marketing tactics, their prices. And be honest with yourself... is this a market you can relatively easily get a foot hold in?

Choose an online marketing method and business model

If you have a talent for communication, and some expertise on a subject, then writing and consulting can be for you. If you don't, you can still make money online with affiliate marketing, and possibly selling on Amazon, eBay, Etsy, and other auction and sales websites. (Keep in mind, if you are selling real, tangible goods, they need to be small and light! You do live in an RV, with limited storage, and you'll need packing materials, and access to a post office.)

What is Affiliate marketing?

Essentially, it is selling other people's products or services, for a commission. There are many ways to use affiliate marketing, as an additional sales venue for your niche market, or as a stand alone business model. Using the dog training example, you could put affiliate links to products, such as training collars, dog food, dog toys and books, on your website. As you promote yourself and your own services, you can also promote supporting products with affiliate links, and make money that way.

As an affiliate marketer, you could also have blogs and websites devoted to product reviews, linking the products with your affiliate links. Many affiliate marketers using this strategy use PPC (pay per click advertising on Google, Yahoo and other search engines) to gain a spot at the top of search engine results, to drive traffic to their websites. IMHO, paying for PPC ads hardly ever seems to pay off, unless the items you are trying to sell have a very good profit margin. A You Tube channel devoted to product reviews can work; as you set up your motorhome or trailer for your new mobile lifestyle, document your progress, and link to products, such as solar panels, wifi and cell equipment, in the video description. This could also be a venue for affiliate marketing involving travel and RV park memberships. You can also use You Tube to promote affiliate marketing involving online services and digital products, or any other item you can review. The Amazon affiliate program has very low commissions, but the advantage is that they stock just about anything in the world you can promote, and just about everyone in the world has purchased something from Amazon, so there is a trust factor. You can also promote affiliate links through social media; be cautious with this, you do not want to be perceived as a spammer. Social media venues that focus on photos, such as Pinterest, can be appropriate for this.

Another way to make money, photography, art and music

If you are living in an RV, you can think about art in the context of what can you do on your laptop. There is a market for royalty free images to use on websites, book and CD covers, tee shirts, royalty free video clips, royalty free music for You Tube videos, TV commercials, video productions, and more. You also need to consider what kind of photographs and video clips will sell to other people, selling stuff on the web; photos and videos that evoke a mood, such as joy or success, or portray subjects such as medical and business professionals, music, online activity, sell well.

You can have a lot of creative and artistic license, just about anything you can imagine will have a place. The thing is, your profit margin on each sale may be quite small, so be prepared to produce a lot of work, like hundreds or thousands of clips. You need a good camera, with high definition. For video, you will also need good video software, and a computer with a fast processor, to mix high definition, full HD or 4K clips. If you are traveling in your RV, you can plan trips around scenic areas, and you may even be able to take your travel expenses as a business expense. If you want to do music clips, you will need good recording equipment, or music software to produce work digitally. There are quite a few websites already established where you can sell your royalty free work, just web search "royalty free images" "royalty free music" "royalty free video" to find some. It should be free to join and start selling, *but read the user agreements, to see if any site wants exclusivity; be sure it is OK to sell your work elsewhere, and be sure not to give your copyrights away!* It is best to put your work out on as many platforms as possible, meaning, sell your photos and video clips on as many websites as you can manage.

In this day and age of digital photography and videography, you could also do wedding and special event photography, and plan your trips around those jobs. You could even offer to do You Tube video reviews of RV parks or tourist attractions, in exchange for some time there.

Tee Shirts and Other Swag

If you have some artistic talent, a sense of humor, and a keen sense of what is happening now, you can make a little extra cash online with print on demand tee shirts, coffee mugs, refrigerator magnets and the like. Political and contemporary entertainment satire, jumping on the latest scandals and controversies can be hot sellers. Just be very, very careful not to infringe on any copyrighted material or logos, use celebrity images without authorization, or say anything that could be construed as defamatory, libel or threatening to life. Two very popular sites to launch such swag are *cafepress.com* and *zazzle.com*. Of course, in order to sell this stuff, you will need to get onto the social networks, stuff some keywords into your titles for the search engines, and maybe do an online press release. Nothing sells itself!

Self Publishing

There are a few different platforms to self publish your writing, without giving away your copyrights. The best genres for writing are non-fiction, how-to type books, but other genres can also be lucrative, it just depends on your talent, and your marketing ability. In addition to having some skill and talent as a writer, you need to have some basic word processing skills, and the ability to format the book the way the online self publishing platform requires; for a paperback or hard cover, that's usually a PDF document, formatted to the trim size of the book. I use Open Office for word processing, it's free, and you can instantly convert your document to PDF by clicking an icon on the tool bar. Also, you can upload the .odf document straight into the Lulu.com converter, to create an ebook through their website). For publishing ebooks, it could be several different types of formats. (You can often find someone on the **_Fiverr.com_** website willing to format an ebook for you for just $5). You may also want to hone your Photoshop skills, to create your own book covers. (Once again, you may find someone to do that for you on Fiverr.com, or some other website). Some *popular online self publishing websites are* **_Lulu.com_** *and* **_CreateSpace.com_**, *as well as* **_Xlibris.com_** *and* **_iUniverse.com_**. **_Amazon Kindle_** *is also a very powerful and popular sales platform for you book.* Lulu.com and Amazon Kindle are two of the best websites for publishing ebooks; Kindle gets them up on Amazon, and Lulu will get you ebook up on iBook for Apple devices, as well as several other ebook platforms.

Another way to make money writing is to write articles for others. Blog owners are constantly looking for "fresh content" to post on their sites. The optimum length of a blog article is around 400-500 words. *There are a lot of websites for freelance writers, such as* **_Scripted.com_**, **_Elance.com_**, **_UpWork.com_**, **_Writeraccess.com_**, *and more, just search "hire freelance writer" to find some, and sign up!*One very important note, if you are writing blog articles for yourself or for others, it is vital you learn the principles of SEO (search engine optimization) and the current levels of optimum keyword density. Getting ranked on the search engines is the whole point of having a website, especially one that is intended to make money.

Consulting

If you have expertise and authority in a field, such as counseling, car mechanic, advice nursing, computer trouble shooting, tarot or psychic reading, or anything else, there are also online platforms for pay-per-minute phone lines, web chat and video chat. These sites are generally free to get started, and collect a percentage of what you charge. Sites like **_Keen.com, LivePerson.com, Kasamba.com, JustAnswer.com_** are popular, but there are others. One note, you'll need a pretty solid internet connection and the GBs to stream, and also a good cell phone connection to make this work.

Computer Related Jobs

You can also work as a freelance computer expert; any and all aspects of website design, script writing, mobile developers, programming, SEO, marketing, troubleshooting, these skills are in high demand. You can find freelance work on websites like **_Freelancer.com, Guru.com, Elance.com, UpWork.com_** and others. These sites are international, you will not only be able to find work "virtually" all over the world, but you will also be competing with other freelancers from all over the world, many of whom will work for a fraction of what Americans will. Make your online resume and thumbnail picture exceptional, and your rates competitive, emphasizing that you are a native English speaker, and easy to work with.

App Development

Everyone wants apps, for everything, these days! App development takes specialized code writing skills, and if you have those, go for it. If you don't, there are some work arounds you can use to get some apps up, especially on **Google Android**. (FYI, Apple iPhone and iPad apps are more difficult; you need to have a Mac, even if you open an Apple developer account, you can not upload your apps without a Mac computer.) Just like selling royalty free photos, music or video clips, you'll need to upload dozens, or maybe even hundreds of apps, to make a living.

Some of the work arounds for simple apps, when you don't know code are:

#1: Set up a Word Press blog, with a "responsive" or "fluid" theme, which will automatically adjust to mobile screen sizes. This website should be somehow workable for an app, such as a training course, arrange the posts and pages as an ebook, an interactive discussion forum, etc. You can open an AdMob account, to place mobile ads on your app, but be aware, Google won't allow you to place both AdMob and AdSense on the same app/website, so choose one. You could also place Amazon or other affiliate links on site. Once your Word Press is set up, go on Fiverr.com, and find someone to convert your website into an app. There will be dozens of sellers, willing to convert your website into an app for $5-10. Then simply upload your app to **Google Play**. If you need to update the app, you simply update your Word Press.

#2: If you want to develop games, create music, video or ebook apps, and have some skill with writing html5, you can download the free Intel XDK software. This is a "cloud" based software, so you'll need a good internet connection. It can also burn up some GBs, depending on what you are uploading. It's pretty easy to learn if you have some computer saavy and coding skill, and the help forum is generally pretty helpful. If you don't have the skills, it's possible to find someone on Fiverr, UpWork, Guru.com or **CodeCanyon.net** or other freelancing sites, to write a script for you, which you can use as a template. Just import the code, and modify it slightly to create different apps.

Word Press

I use Word Press blogs. There are many attractive and functional, free Word Press "themes", and also low cost paid themes, making it very easy to create the look and functionality you want. Choose a "responsive" or "fluid" theme, as these will automatically adjust in size to mobile phone and tablet screens. Word Press makes it super easy to update your website, add users, such as guest writers, and customize with "plugins". Plugins can do many things, such as automatically sending new posts to social media, help with search engine optimization, create an online store, a discussion forum, and much more. Some of the plugins I use routinely are SEO Ultimate, WP Simple AdSense Insertion, NextScripts Social Networks Auto-Poster, Delete Pending Comments, and RSS Via Shortcode for Page & Post. (I use RSS via Shortcode to import my eBay affiliate RSS feed). You may have to experiment with different plugins, installing and uninstalling until you find the one you really need, and that really work. If you have problems with your Word Press not working the way it should, you can get low cost tech help on Fiverr.com.

Web Hosting for Your Sites

There are many companies providing hosting for websites. Things to consider, besides price, is if the web host has good customer service and solid up time (look for online reviews), and also, if they provide SSL certificates, for taking credit cards. (You can use Pay Pal as a credit card processor, but they'll require an SSL certificate.) Also, website templates or a control panel to install Word Press.

What If I Can't Write?

There are a few ways around this; you can have "guest bloggers" write articles for you, you can buy articles, and you can "spin" articles. "Spinning" an article involves rewriting an article, making enough change to avoid the search engine "duplicate content" filters.

Other bloggers and website owners, who are in the same genre as you, may write an article for you, in exchange for a link to their sites. This can be double edged, you'll get content for your site, but linking to a lower ranking website might lower your rankings. You can pay people to write for you, but this can be costly, if the writer is a native English speaker who can actually write, or it can hurt you, if you go for the 3rd World bargains from sites like Fiverr.com. Often, these budget writers will simply copy and paste from other websites, and "duplicate content" will hurt you, both with the search engines, and also as possible copyright infringement. Spin these articles, changing enough words and phrases to seem like "fresh content" to the search engines. And of course, you can teach yourself better writing and communication skills!

Online Payments

The easiest way to take online payments is through *Pay Pal*. You can easily create Pay Pal sales buttons to place on your website, and many online sales platforms, like eBay, will pay you monthly through Pay Pal. Pay Pal takes a small percentage from the seller for each transaction, but that fee can be taken off your taxes as a business expense. One thing to note, if you are taking credit card payments through your website, via Pay Pal, you will need to set up your website with an SSL certificate. Your web hosting company should be able to do that for you, free or for a nominal cost. When you are shopping for a web host, look to see if they provide an SSL certificate with their hosting plans.

You can also get a Pay Pal debit card, which you can use like any other debit card, and you can get a Pay Pal card reader for your smart phone, to take debit and credit card transactions if you are selling in "real life", such as at a flea market or craft fair. Pay Pal is a must for an online business.

Combine different online money making platforms

There are many different venues with which to market your products and services online. Using the dog training business as an example, you can write and self publish an ebook and a paperback on your particular niche, and get those up on Amazon. Lulu.com is a good way to get your ebook to iBook (Apple products) and other non-Kindle ebook platforms. You could also self produce a video, on DVD or for download (you can do this on CreateSpace.com). You will also launch an informative and attractive blog, incorporating the principles of successful, search engine friendly SEO, with direct links to purchase your book, your video, as well as some affiliate links to buy other related products, such as a dog training supplies and books. You can also set up an online chat, Skype or a phone line, to give individual training sessions, for a pay per minute fee. Set this blog up with a responsive theme, and turn it into an app. Once you start making contacts and creating networks online, you could schedule some in person training seminars in different locations, and use that to map out your trips, and use your traveling expenses as a business expense. Don't forget to make videos for You Tube, Vimeo and other online video sites, to create an audience for your products and services, and drive traffic to your site. That is just the beginning...

SEO (Search Engine Optimization)

I have mentioned "SEO" several times, now it's time for an explanation. SEO stands for "search engine optimization". Search engines, such as Google, Bing, Yahoo, and even the internal search engines for eBay, Etsy, Facebook, Amazon, You Tube and other social media sites, use "algorythms" (formulas) to find the articles and items people are searching for.

First of all, algorythms use "keywords". These are the search terms people are using to find what they want. Using the dog training example again, you would want to use the search terms people are using, such as "dog training", or better yet, go deeper with your niche, "bloodhound training" or "training a pitbull". You would put these terms into your titles; the titles for your blog posts and social media posts, your You Tube videos, and also, your books, if you are writing. Also sprinkle the keywords throughout your articles; don't go overboard, or else the search engine algorythm might perceive your work as "spamming keywords" to game the system.

I have noticed on You Tube, many people do not understand the concept of keywords, and their value in allowing people to find their videos. They might title their videos with "Season 2, Episode 3, I Get Stuck!!!" That might be intriguing for their friends and close fans, but useless for someone searching for a video on how to get a travel trailer out of the mud. A better title would be, "RV Trailer Stuck in Mud How To". Also, put keywords into the description section. With You Tube, if your channel is monetized, you might also consider keywords aimed at the AdSense advertising; you do not make money on You Tube because you have lots of views or likes, but by how many people click through to the ads. With our "stuck in the mud" example, keywords like "RV road service", "RV insurance", "winches", "4x4 truck" might bring up ads of interest to your viewers.

This concept also goes for social media and blog posts, as well as book titles. Once again, the dog training example; let's say, you write a blog and/or social media post about how you got your poodle to stop the habit of food aggression against other dogs. A title like, "Fluffy Stop That!" is useless. A title like, "How to Stop Food Aggression My Poodle", includes search-able keywords and phrases.

You can search the phrase "keyword tool" to find online tools to help you find out what the most popular keywords are for your genre. For example, I typed in "dog training" to an online keyword tool, and came up with the top phrases, "dog training collars", "dog training tips", "dog training classes". You can use these keyword ideas to write articles and posts, and also, as ideas for products and services to promote and sell.

Another aspect to SEO is popularity; how many other websites are linked to your site, and how many social media shares do you have? This aspect of SEO is tricky, and not easily manipulated or faked. You may come across online services, often originating out of India or Indonesia, offering SEO linking services. This is popular on Fiverr. Don't go for it! Search engines such as Google can sense when links are "spun" and faked, and this will bring down your search engine rankings, not help. I'd also caution against buying You Tube video views, likes and comments. Also, social media shares, such as when someone shares a link to one of your articles on Facebook, also count with the search engines. If you are selling on Amazon or eBay, positive reviews count. Once again, be very cautious with online services offering to sell you reviews, likes or shares. If you are on Fiverr.com, you may notice people selling "real" shares, likes, views and friends. They are most likely not "real", but computer generated with spam-bot programs. Also, search engines and social media sites can track by "IP addresses", and links,likes and reviews being "spammed" from a single IP, or originating from 3rd World countries, will be detected, and count against you.

Social Media Marketing

Social media sites like Facebook, Google+, Twitter, You Tube, Pinterest, LinkedIn, and many, many others, can bring you a lot of business, if done right. It also can become tedious and time consuming. What you need for social media success is a combination of "viral" posts, and social media posting tools, like Buffer.com or HootSuite.com. There are others too, do a little searching, and see what matches your needs. A subscription to Buffer.com or HootSuite.com can be as little as $10 a month, and with it, you can simultaneously post to Facebook, Twitter, Google+, Pinterest, LinkedIn, and other social media sites, and even schedule posts for the future. Imagine, you can spend a few hours to schedule posts for the next 2 weeks, freeing up your time to do real work! These online tools can also help you to figure out the posting times most likely to be seen, tell you which posts are the most popular, and more.

In order to create popular posts on social media, you have to avoid coming across as straight up advertising. "Spamming" other people's posts with ads and links to your business is not cool. It's a turn off, which may cause people to turn against you, and report you for spamming. The right way to do it? Create content that is informative, uplifting, and humorous. The dog training business is a perfect example; who on Facebook doesn't like cute puppies? Creating "memes" (those pictures with the sayings on them) of cute puppies, with your website discreetly in the corner, then a little blurb like, "Keep that puppy cute, he needs training! How to article here" with your website URL, is the right way to do it. Give people a cute picture to share, with a discreet link. Let's say you are starting a mobile mechanic business; how about videos of the highway patrol and other roadside good samaritans, saving critters, with a description saying, "Good job guys! I'd do the same! If you need help on the road, just contact me!" It doesn't have to be all puppies and kitties, the point is, post informative articles from your websites, post informative product reviews with affiliate links, inspiring, funny and shareable "memes", photos and videos, that will catch people's attention, without coming across like "advertising". "Friend" and follow others with success in your genre, and watch for their most popular posts, videos and memes to get ideas.

With Facebook and Google+, you can create pages for your business, and you should do that. In fact, many small businesses just use a Facebook business page, without building a website. It's easy to get started, but if you need help, you can hire someone from Fiverr.com for very little, to help you set it up. Facebook also offers advertising of your posts; this can be a very cost effective, and Facebook allows your to target your audience very specifically. You can see what your demographic is, let's say, the largest group to respond to your posts are women, aged 35-55, at 65% of your audience. Using the dog training example, let's say you want to promote a post regarding an online training seminar you are going to have about food aggression in dogs. You can target women 35-55, with an interest in dogs, and fine tune the interests, with keywords like "dog training", "dog aggression" and "food aggression in dogs". You can spend very little, let's say $10-20, and have that post reach thousands of people with that specific interest, and if it creates just one or two leads, it can have paid off.

Another important factor in social media marketing is joining groups; use your business related keywords to find groups, as well as joining groups related to your personal interests. You may have scheduled posts through Buffer.com or

HootSuit.com for the next two weeks, but every day, log into your social media accounts, and share your best posts to your groups. Be very careful not to spam ads, you may get kicked out of the group. Simply like and comment on the posts of others, and share your most informative and fun posts, that have a direct correlation on the focus of the group. This is one of the most effective ways to get post likes and shares, and shares are free advertising!

Staying Connected Online

If you are traveling, and especially, if you like to go deep off the beaten path into the wilderness, you won't have an internet connection. Simple fact. You won't. *Most fulltime RVers go with Verizon, because they have the widest coverage, and the strongest signals, but check your area coverage maps.* That is another thing to consider; certain activities online can burn up the GBs faster than others... streaming video, online chat, and Skype will put you close to the edge of your plan faster than anything. Uploading a lot of audio and video will also burn up the GBs. So be aware, and keep track of what you need to do when, the coverage maps, and your limits on data. Of course, you can supplement some of your online activity, and make your data plan go further, by using public WiFi connections, like at Starbuck's or McDonald's, public libraries or at the campground. It is a good idea, to use, or subscribe to, a "VPN Tunnel". VPN stands for, virtual private network, and it will encrypt your activity when on public networks. The Firefox browser has VPN plug ins available, and you can also subscribe to VPN services.

In addition to looking at cell coverage maps, a good thing to do, especially in rural areas, is to look up where the cell towers are. Getting as close as possible to the tower will ensure a good signal. **CellReception.com** has cell tower maps, and there are other sites too. Another thing to consider, park as high up as possible, and line of sight, being in a rocky valley can block a cell signal.

Wifi Boosters

You can also get a cellphone signal booster, designed for a car or truck, which can bring up the number of bars you have, either on your phone, or your internet wifi device. **WeBoost is a very popular brand of cell booster.** This will have an exterior antennae to put on your roof, as well as an interior booster, on which you will connect your device. These can be pricey, but also can be well worth it in order to stay connected. I have a 4G WeBoost, and a fiberglass antenna on the roof, and it definitely makes the difference between a weak signal and a better one, when I need it.

But what about satellite internet? A lot of people think the logical solution to the internet problem is to get satellite internet; unfortunately, at this time, that is not as practical as it sounds. Satellite internet is actually slower than 3G/4G, and you will need to spend quite a bit of money for the equipment (new, at least $1,500) and it can take up a lot of room, like an entire shelf in a cabinet. Most satellite internet providers are geared to stationary set ups, and will charge more for mobile applications. It is absolutely do-able, but if you are looking to live in an RV in order to live more affordably, satellite internet may not be the answer.

Offline Ways to Make Money

There are quite a few "real life" ways to make money, while living in an RV (or anywhere). Once again, you need to pursue these goals with creativity, focus and determination.

Workamping

You may have heard of "workamping" (work camping). This is an opportunity to work at a camp ground, in exchange for a space, and often, a small wage. Often, workamping gigs prefer couples; they get two for one that way. And, this is one form of employment where the older RVer and couples may have an advantage over the younger fulltimer and the solo. These jobs often do not pay enough cash to actually live on, (even though you get the free space) and were created with a retiree in mind, someone with a pension or social security check to cover most of their food and personal items. But if you don't have a lot of bills, and can live simply, a younger fulltimer is definitely in the running, especially for the jobs which might be more physical, such as landscaping, clearing brush and construction, or jobs that require more computer saavy. You can find workamping opportunities all over; at private camp grounds, as well as state and national parks. There are many forums and websites devoted to workamping, and web searching "workamping" is the best place to start, if this interests you. There are also magazines, such as *Workamper News*, which also has the website, **www.**workamper.com . There are other websites, like **www.workampingjobs.com** and others. Just search engine the term, "workamping" to find online resources.

Working at Amazon

A workamping gig for a younger, single person might be working for Amazon; bet you didn't know, that Amazon hires RVers to pick and pack at their warehouses, during the Christmas buying season! I say this is well suited to a younger person because, the work at Amazon requires long hours, and a certain level of health and physical fitness. If you are disabled or elderly, this is **not** for you!

The "Amazon Camper Force" typically will work 10 hours a day, four days a week, and this involves standing for long hours at a packing station, or running around the warehouse (at least 5 miles per day) picking items, packing boxes, gift wrapping, and other warehouse shipping work. *It is physical work.* Amazon will rent out an entire RV park for their workers, so you get your space for free too, as well as the hourly pay. They have locations all over the country. Amazon has a good reputation for treating their work force fairly and well, with better than average pay, and they work to to make being a part of the Camper Force rewarding and fun.

Temp Agencies

If you are planning on visiting certain cities and urban areas and staying for a while, you might consider signing up with the local temp agencies. You will need to have a local address (the RV park) and fill out an application and have an interview, to determine what type of work you are suited for. Once you do get a job or two, and get some good feedback, you might be able to transfer your application information to the affiliated temp agency in the next town on your itinerary.

Agricultural Jobs

This includes working on farms and ranches, game reserves, landscaping, but also, working the rodeo circuit, state fairs and Christmas tree sales. Check the workamper websites and magazines for leads.

Property Caretaking Jobs

Property caretaking jobs are definitely available, with resorts and retreats, ranches, house sitting for the wealthy, and more. You can explore caretaking jobs through magazines such as The Caretaker's Gazette, (*website at caretaker.org*) Also web search "property caretaker jobs" for more websites and forums that may generate leads.

Property caretaking could also include a "night security" gig. You might find a local business, RV or car sales lot, or a construction site that would be willing to let you park at night, in exchange for keeping an eye on things, and calling the police if necessary. These situations are generally informal, "off the books" unpaid arrangements, a simple exchange for a place to park at night.

Flea Markets, Art Fairs, Renaissance Faires, Farmer's Markets and Special Events

Selling on the weekends can be absolutely ideal for a fulltime RVer. Many flea markets, fairs and special events will allow the vendors to park their rig for free, or a nominal fee, during the event. In addition to selling, there are other opportunities, such as collecting gate fees, cleaning up, performing arts, and more, so this could be an ideal opportunity for an artist, actor, musician or psychic reader. Keep in mind, you may need to sell small, light weight items, as storage in an RV is limited. You will need tables, a chair, and an awning, which will need to find space for in the RV, or you may have to tow a small moving trailer behind your Class A, B or C motorhome. Clark's Flea Market Guide has up to date listings of flea markets around the country.

Flea Markets, Art Fairs, Renaissance Faires, and Farmer's Markets are also great venues if you are an artist or crafter. You can also sell your arts and crafts items on websites like *Etsy.com* and *eBay.com* as well as possibly selling on social media. Always consider, you will need space in your RV to store these items, and also, be close to a post office to ship online sales.

Where do you find wholesale goods to sell?

One fast and easy place to start is eBay; search "wholesale lots" and "wholesale lots free shipping". Also, web search "wholesale lots" "flea market". You will find many websites selling wholesale lots, which might involve pallets of returned store merchandise, overstocks, or new stuff from China. If you have a home base city where you can rent a storage unit, then buying pallets and truckloads might be the way to go. But if you don't, then buying smaller quantities of smaller, light weight items, such as jewelry, knives, sunglasses, clothing and DVDs, might be necessary. Also consider the shipping; you will need to stay put, perhaps for a month, waiting on new shipments of sales stock. Shipping can be very costly, so avoid having the items shipped once to your mail forwarding address, then again to your current location.

If you're working flea markets, make sure you have plenty

of change, ones and five dollar bills! Another advantage to flea markets, festivals and fairs, is that it is mostly a cash business, no need for credit cards, Pay Pal, direct deposits, or pay checks. Your customers will simply be handing over cash!

Don't put all your eggs in one basket...

Unless you have a pension, or a really secure, well paying job you can take with you, a combination of different money making strategies might be a good idea; an online business, combined with workamping or caretaking, flea marketing and festivals combined with temp agencies, so on and so forth, might be the best bet to keep the RV rolling, with gas money and places to park. The economy can change quickly these days, be prepared to move and change with it!

What Type of RV is Right for YOU?

There are two types of RVs, towables (trailers) and motorhomes, and there are several classes within these two general classifications. Which one is right for you? That depends on your what type of lifestyle you want to achieve, how much money and what type of resources you have to work with, and what's available on the market.

If you plan on workamping and living in campgrounds, a towable might be the right choice; you will be stationary for perhaps months at a time, and can use your truck to get around and run errands. But if your plan is to move around the country frequently, then a motorhome might be the right choice.

A motorhome is a motor vehicle chassis and living space all in one. This is what most people think of when they hear "RV". There are three types, or classes of motorhome:

The Class A Motorhome (and I will also include bus conversions here).

This is the type of RV that looks like a bus. Class A's can be fueled by either gas or diesel. A gas fueled RV will generally be less expensive to buy and maintain, but a diesel RV will have more torque for climbing hills, better braking and suspension and can carry and tow more weight. The "diesel pusher" is a very desirable model, which will hold it's value better than any other. The diesel pusher is so called because the diesel engine is in the back, giving it extra power and fuel efficiency. The Class A can range in length from 26' to 45'.

Ironically, while the Class A is often the most expensive to buy new, you can often find good deals on used ones; a 10 year old Class A, that was originally a mid-priced model, may go for significantly less than a comparable Class B or C. That is because they are usually bigger, can't go very far off road, can't be as easily used for urban stealth camping, and have poor gas mileage. The Class A RV generally has a low bottom clearance, so it does not do as well on rutted dirt roads. You can't just park it anywhere, you'll be taking up 2-3 spaces in any parking lot, and you simply won't be able to maneuver in certain places.

Of course, there are advantages to the Class A, including the fact that there seem to be quite a few older ones out there with an affordable price tag. Also, they have more space inside, more storage capacity, and are designed for comfortable living. They come with built in generators, large tanks, nice cabinets, queen size beds, as well as fold out sofas, reclining chairs, and dinettes. A Class A would be a good choice for an older person, who needs accessibility, or a couple or a family with kids. They are also good for those who are running a small business on the road, due to their roominess, comfort and storage capacity.

The Class B Motorhome (and van conversions)

This is the type of RV that looks like a van, with a higher roof. There are both gas and diesel, and they range in length from 16' to 21'. These days, it seems the Class B is often the priciest used RV; that's because their small size, maneuverability, van like appearance and fair gas mileage makes them today's top choice for urban stealth camping and boondocking. You could live in the city in a Class B, and find parking at night on a quiet side street, industrial area or in a friend's driveway. You can also go across country, with fairly decent gas mileage, boondock and stealth camp along the way.

The big downside to a Class B is the same as it's biggest advantage; it's small size. Don't underestimate how small it is to live in one of these! Some Class B's have bathrooms, and some don't. The ones that do generally have a sort of all in one plastic closet, with the toilet and shower as one unit. They have small fresh, grey and black tanks, making frequent dumping and filling necessary. There really isn't much outside storage, like in a Class A or C, and very minimal inside storage; if you are OK with having, let's say, three tee shirts, two pairs of pants, two pairs of shorts, one or two sweaters, a pair of sneakers and a pair of sandals, maybe a jacket plus some underwear, you are good to go. But, if you require a more extensive wardrobe, a library of books, or a lot of tools for your work, rethink the Class B. Also, the kitchens are very small; generally a two burner stove, and a mini fridge, with a tiny sink. If you love gourmet cooking, once again, a Class B might not be for you. But, if you are the adventurous type who likes to travel light, and have a real need to boondock and especially, urban stealth camp, the Class B might be your ticket to freedom.

The Class C Motorhome

This is the type of motorhome that looks like a giant camper turtle shell was placed over a big van. Similar in size to Class A, but it has a sleeping space over the cab and are often available in smaller sizes, lengths from 20' to 32'. Like the Class B, a used Class C motorhome may sell for more than a comparable Class A, for many of the same reasons, but very old Class Cs are often cheap to buy, because they tend to develop leaks in the cab over, and other structural problems. The smaller Class C's are (a little) more maneuverable and parkable than a Class A, and the small ones might get away with urban stealth camping. The Class C can travel most roads, and has a much storage room and amenities as a comparably sized Class A. This may be the way to go if you have children, kids love the overhead beds! If you are a solo or a couple, you could use either the overhead bed, or the regular bed, and convert the other bed to extra storage. This may be a good choice if you plan to make some extra money at flea markets and fairs.

Truck Campers

The advantages of a truck camper are many; you can put it on a 4x4 truck, and go deep off road. They are easy to park, and get decent gas mileage. You can keep your camper (and any modifications you made) and put it on a different truck, rather than having to sell the whole thing. The disadvantages are like those of a Class B; may or may not have a bathroom, and if it does, it's very small and minimal. Minimal kitchen, and a minimal amount of storage (although some of the newer truck campers feature slide outs, to make more room). They also have small fresh, grey and black tanks, making frequent dumping and filling necessary. On top of that, you need to exit the camper, in order to gain access to the truck, and drive away; not a good thing in an emergency situation, such as, you are boondocking or stealth camping, and you find yourself under attack by a crazed meth addict, or a highway bandit! Surprisingly, a new truck camper will cost you as much, or even more, than a much larger and better equiped travel trailer, and you might be surprised at the cost of a used truck camper, although there are some very good deals to be had for these versatile units.

Towable RVs (trailers)

We all know what a trailer is, and there are advantages to towing rather than driving. If you are workamping, staying in places for weeks or months at a time, or just need to reduce your rent, a trailer could be a good choice. Depending on the size of your trailer, you will need a truck, SUV, or van, equipped to tow, which you can use to drive around on an everyday basis. Except for the very smallest travel trailers, a 3/4 ton tow vehicle is the norm, you may even need a one ton truck for the largest 5th wheels and travel trailers. **And make sure your truck has a tow package.** *A tow package is more than just a hitch receptacle; a truck, van or SUV with a factory installed tow package will also have an upgraded transmission, brakes, suspension and drive train, designed for hauling, and the wiring for the towable's brake lights. It is vital that you check your tow vehicle's towing capacity, and make sure it matches your towable!*

I'll break down the different types of towables. There are three main types:

The Fifth Wheel Trailer

This is the type of trailer that has the extension that goes over the bed of the pick up truck. This is because this type of trailer has a particular type of hitch, similar to those used on a big rig truck, that sits in the bed of the pick up. This type of hitch, and the fact that the trailer sits over the truck, almost like one unit, makes for easier towing and maneuvering. Also, this extension gives the 5th wheel trailer a two level floor plan, with the bedroom on top, and higher ceilings than any other type of RV. (If you are very tall, this might be the RV for you.) 5th Wheels have plenty of storage, inside and out, full size kitchens, full size bathrooms (some have two bathrooms) and make a great, fulltime home for families with children. They range in size from 20' to 40', but the larger 5th wheels seem more common. There are some older and smaller 5th wheels (like 18'-22', from the 80s and 90s) that can be had for cheap and restored, that could be pulled by a smaller pick up. The disadvatanges of the 5th wheel is it's size and height; you really need to watch the overhead clearance, especially at gas stations. Also, your full size truck bed will be filled with the 5th wheel hitch, leaving very little room for anything else, and you can't put a shell on it. But that 5th wheel hitch also makes you much less susceptible to jack knifing and fish tailing, thus, it is a safer and more stable tow than a travel trailer.

The Travel Trailer

Typically smaller and lighter than a 5th wheel, the travel trailer has a single level floor plan. There are several types of travel trailers. Starting with the smallest:

The Teardrop has no bathroom, no tanks, or very small tanks, and just enough room to sleep two people. The kitchen is actually outside; there is a hatch that opens up, with a cook stove and some storage, but no refrigerator, and maybe a dishpan for a sink. The new, modern Teardrops, such as a T@b brand trailer, often do have an inside, micro-mini kitchen, and may have a micro-mini bathroom, placed at the expense of any storage that might be had. The advantage to a Teardrop is nearly any fullsized (or even small sized) car can pull it. These are not suited for fulltime living, unless you are really OK with always using the campground bathroom facilities, or, you have a place to park it, such as in the backyard of family or friends, and you can use their bathroom and kitchen.

The Travel Trailer, which can range in length from 15' to 35', has all the amenities you will need; depending on the size of the trailer, you will have a full sized (or nearly full sized) bathroom, a full sized kitchen (though counter space may be limited) sofa, dinette, and bedroom (although in the smallest travel trailers, the bed may be in the same room as everything else, with no separating wall).

A third type of travel trailer is the **Toy Hauler**; these are recognized by the fact that the entire back wall is one big door, which folds down as a ramp. They are designed to haul your ATV, motorcycles, and other "toys". They generally have a bed (for the kids) which will come down from the ceiling in the garage area, and another bedroom towards the front. Despite their rough and tumble origins, many Toy Haulers are quite luxurious inside, with full amenities. A Toy Hauler is a great choice if you like to travel and stay in areas for a week or more at a time, and want a base camp while you explore on your ATV or motorcycle. This could also be a very good choice for someone who is traveling with sales goods for flea markets and art fairs, as the garage area can also be used for storage. *Toy haulers can be either a 5th wheel, or a travel trailer.*

The last type of towable I will cover is the **Folding Camping Trailer**. Like the Teardrop, these are very small, and as the name indicates, they fold up (and down) meaning you will need to fold and unfold every time you stop and need to set up. Like the Teardrop, they also generally don't have bathrooms, and minimal kitchens. Also, they have tent canvas siding, so they are not suitable for colder climates. One advantage, they are light weight, can be towed by a large car or small truck, and can go deeper off road than most trailers. But overall, the Folding Tent Trailer is the least suitable for fulltime living.

A Travel Trailer is a nice choice for a couple, or a small family, depending on the size of the trailer. Single people, especially women, may have trouble handling the heavy trailer hitch and sway bars. Be realistic with your physical abilities. **Once again, you will need a good tow vehicle, preferably a 3/4 to one ton ton truck or SUV** (except for the smallest trailers) with a factory installed tow package. It is vital that you check your tow vehicle's towing capacity, and make sure it matches your towable! Many people will first buy the towable they want, then buy the truck to match the trailer's weight. Of course, if you already have a tow vehicle with a tow package, find a towable that will match your truck, as far as weight and your truck's towing capacity.

Motorhomes vs. Towables

The type of RV you choose is a personal preference, dependent on your needs and your goals, but there are some basic differences that can help you decide.

The Pros of a Motorhome

Except for the truck camper, you do not need to leave the motorhome to start your engine.
You don't have to worry about hitching a trailer by yourself.
You are not going to fish tail or jack knife like a trailer might.
It's easier to set up, no hitching and unhitching.
Many motorhomes have self leveling jacks, so there is no need to place blocks or levelers under the wheels.
You can tow a small, economical car, or have a bike or motorcycle on the back.

The Cons of a Motorhome

If it winds up in the shop, you may need to find somewhere

else to live. (Although many RV shops will allow you to "boondock").
Motorhomes tend to be more expensive, even when factoring in a tow vehicle for the towable.
Motorhomes generally have less living space than an equivalent length towable.
Motorhomes depreciate faster.
When towing a car, you cannot back up, and you have the cost and maintenance of two vehicles.

The Pros of a Towable

They are less expensive and hold their value longer.
They have more living space than a similar sized motorhome.
You can leave the towable at the campsite, and take the tow vehicle on errands.
If your tow vehicle is in the shop, you can still live in the towable.

The Cons of A Towable

Towing and hitching/unhitching towables can be a headache, and physicallly difficult for some people.
For the longer towables, parking and finding campsites can be a problem.
Tow vehicles, like 3/4 ton and one ton trucks, can be really expensive, even used.
The gas mileage on a large truck, towing a trailer will be no better than a motorhome, and without towing, your gas mileage will still be bad.
Towables can jack knife or fish tail, causing very serious accidents.

Determining Your Lifestyle and Comfort Levels

You may have been watching some of the young, hip, urban stealth campers on You Tube, living free on the streets of big, expensive cities in a Class B, while they pursue school, or some cool, hip career. They make it look so easy! So glamorous! So anti-social in a really cool way! Maybe, but hold up, reality check.... Knock, knock, knock, the glare of a flashlight... it's the cops! "You can't park here. License and registration..." Maybe this time, you get off without a ticket, or maybe not. Bang, bang bang! "Gimme all you got!" Oh no! It's a meth addicted gang banger with a mental illness, brandishing a weapon! What do you do? It can, and does happen. You really have to think about this. If your plan is urban stealth camping, you really have to look at your environment, and map out the safest, most low profile places you can find, areas where *no one* goes at night. If you are urban stealth camping, you will need black out curtains, and probably will have to call it an early night; lights attract attention, it *can not* look like there is anyone inside that van! Oh, and no running the heater or air conditioner, those make noise!

Or maybe you have been watching the adventures of an environmentally conscious young fellow, driving his Class B across the country, bugging out off grid to the wilderness, fishing for his dinner,   cooking over a fire, nearly freezing to death as he camps out in the Alaska wilderness... really cool, really romantic, but that actually costs money. You will still need to pay for your car insurance, license, registration, gas, and, believe it or not, your chances of actually "bugging out and living off the land" 100% are not that good, so you will at least sometimes have to buy food. How will you support yourself, if you are "off grid"?

Maybe you saw some guy on You Tube, who scored a mold covered, 35' Class A from the 80's with a badly leaking roof and a bad case of mildew, for $500. He's planning on living for free, in the Walmart parking lot. Wow! $500! You think you can score something like that too! You could rebuild it, refurbish it, make it really cool with solar panels, and wind power, and a satellite system... OK, maybe. But really, do you have the construction and mechanical skills to do this? Do you know how hard it is to get rid of mold? Do you realize how expensive tires for an RV cost? Because the tires on your great Craigslist score are undoubtedly dry rotted. Do you have some place where it will be OK to leave this monstrosity all tore up, for months and months, while you fix it, without getting a ticket, or having the neighbors start a petition? If not, rescuing this wreck could cost you a a lot more than you anticipated! And "living for free, at Walmart" is simply not reality.

The same goes for building your dream RV from scratch, building a mobile tiny house, or turning a delivery truck into a stealth camper; all very do-able, but seriously consider your skills levels, your resources, your time, money, and if you have a space to do this, without running into trouble with the neighbors, building code enforcers or the police.

If your goal is to build something from scratch, you can find RV parts, like RV toilets and tanks, but also look into marine parts. Boats use many of the same sort of components, and some that are unique, and might be better suited for your plans. And don't forget, you will be moving, and your tiny house or homemade trailer will be under "earthquake conditions" going 60 mph down the highway! You need to teach yourself the techniques and principles of construction that will ensure durability and safety under these extreme conditions of shake, rattle and roll. A simple hammer and nails approach might lead to disaster. And design it as light as possible, excess weight can also lead to disaster.

Another thing, if you are building your own RV, a very important consideration is *weight distribution*; it is vital that the weight from side to side is even. For instance, it would be a very bad plan to put your tanks (water weighs 8 lbs per gallon) and your kitchen appliances all on one side, and just your bed on the other. If you want to build your own dream RV, please research the design aspect and the principle of weight distribution thoroughly.

I'm not trying to bash your dreams, just throwing in a reality check; you really need to think it out, and be honest with yourself, about your comfort and skill levels, practicality, and resources. Be prepared!

Some deal killers (or serious re-negotiators) on purchasing an RV

Leaky roof, look for evidence of water spots on the ceiling, inside cabinets and closets
Moldy or mildew smell (indicates leaks)
Soft or spongy spots on the floor
Rust
It really looks like a trashed out junker

If the RV you are looking at has been sitting for a long time, the tires are likely dry rotted (very dangerous, and expensive to replace) as well as any other rubber parts. Lubricants can be dried out, causing a potentially dangerous, or expensive, situation. If your RV has a surprisingly low mileage for it's age, it has been sitting in storage! Before you start driving it all over the place, take it immediately to a qualified mechanic, for a full inspection! You will SAVE money in the long run, if you can find the issues and fix them before they become expensive repairs!

So now, we come to the next part of this beginner's guide to an alternative RV lifestyle...

Where to Park It?

The first thing you need to do, after you figure out the type of lifestyle and RV best suited to you, is figure out where you are going to park it. *One important point: if you live somewhere with hot summers or very cold winters, "living for free" on the streets might not be realistic. You can not run an air conditioner without being hooked up to electricity (or running a noisy generator) and keeping warm enough in deep snow might be impossible.*

Sure, you can spend a night or two parking at Walmart, but unhitching it, and even putting out the slide outs (if you have them) will be frowned upon. You are going to have to find a safe place to park it, and unless you have your solar panels set up on the roof, or a generator, you'll have to go with with "full hook ups". (Hook ups are electricity, a water source, and a sewer to dump your waste water). This could be a trailer park, an RV resort, or state or national park campground. If you are workamping, this will be provided for you. If you have your solar set up, or a gas or diesel generator, you can boondock for free on BLM (Bureau of Land Management) land, but if you need to work online, I'd suggest having a 4G cell booster, and checking the cell coverage and cell tower maps for your target area.

Another thing, make sure the ground where you plan to park your is solid and relatively level; if the ground is riddled with gopher holes, there will be a network of tunnels to cave in under you. Don't park it on sand. You can level the trailer with your leveling jacks, but only up to maybe a foot. Find the levelest and most solid and stable patch of ground available to you.

Here are some businesses that may allow overnight parking. But check with individual stores; these days, with so many people looking to RVs as alternative housing, rather than as a "recreational vehicle" for vacationing, some stores are understandably revoking this courtesy, due to abuse by some mobile homeless. Remember, do not over stay your welcome, or abuse your priveleges!

Wal-Mart, Kmart, Target, Sam's Club, Costco, Meijer, Camping World, Cracker Barrel, Lowes, Menards, Flying J Truck Stop, Loves Travel Stop, Pacific Pride Fuel, Petro Truck Stop, Pilot Travel Center, TA Travel Center

During the day, you can park in the back end of just about any big shopping center parking lot (be considerate, and do not block parking for their customers, or you may be asked to leave) the large parking lot of a city park (the police may stop by though, just to make sure you are not camping for the night), or many other places you might find. Just be aware of your size, and don't block the flow of traffic, or cause concern for the neighbors or passersby; stay low profile.

If you have one of the smallest Class Cs, a Class B or a truck camper, your options are even greater, due to your small size, and low profile look. You will be able to simply park on back streets, and lay low for the night. *But be very careful about where, and when, you choose to park!* You may find a safe, quiet suburban neighborhood.... the best plan of action may be, to come in after dark, after most working people are going to bed (let's say, between 9 pm and 11 pm) and park in an area that is not directly in front of anyone's house, like around a corner, alongside of a backyard fence, etc. You might try the back parking lot of a church, in a quiet, suburban neighborhood. Put up your blackout curtains, turn out the lights, and call it a night. When the sun starts to come up, start your engine, and pull quietly away. Rotate your stealth camping areas! Do not become an unwelcome guest!

Another area that might be good for overnight parking is the local industrial area; you know, that part of town with all the auto mechanics, welding and machine shops and stuff, and no residential houses in sight. These areas are mostly abandoned after people get off work, except perhaps for handful of stray dogs, cats and homeless people.

You may also find a hardly used dirt road going off into the brush, in a park, or out in the country, and park for the night. The idea is, to come and go in such a way that you do not attract attention. Of course, there is always "driveway camping" at friends and family. Once again, rotate these around, so as not to wear out your welcome, or attract unwanted attention from neighbors.

One important point, avoid schools! Trying to park your RV at an elementary school or high school at night may get you tagged as some sort of pervert, and colleges and universities can have pretty aggressive security!

If you are a veteran, many outposts of the VFW (Veterans of Foreign Wars) will allow you to park overnight in the parking lot. *Also, there are military campgrounds available for active duty and retired military.*
militarycampgrounds.us *and*
freecampgrounds.com/military.html

Most RV parks will allow you to dump for a fee, usually $5-15. Some truck stops and gas stations also have dump sites, as well as state and county fair grounds, and some highway rest stops. A good plan may be to stay at a campground once very two weeks or so, to dump and fill your tanks, and use their laundry and shower facilities. **One thing you may not know, many state and county fairgrounds also have RV spaces available, for a cheap price.** These were originally put in for events, such as the state fair, when exhibitors come and camp out for the duration. But regular people are also welcome to stay.

A good, online resource for some free camping areas across the country is the "7 in 1 eBook" found on gypsyjournalrv.com You may have to hunt a little for the link, it keeps moving around, but *"The 7 in 1 eBook" covers Free Campgrounds, Fairground Camping, Casino Camping, RV Parks with Wifi, RV Dump Stations, RV "Good Guys", and the authors Favorite Restaurants.* It is not a 100% comprehensive list, but it is definitely a good place to start, and will give you some leads and clues.

Living for "free" in an RV on the streets is not an exact science; every town, city, RV and RVer are different. What is safe and OK in one place, could be illegal and dangerous somewhere else. Everyone needs to find their own comfort level and work out their own strategy, that is in tune with their environment.

I am listing a few website resources here, between the in town and out of town camping, since these can go either way.

<u>Freecampsites.net</u>
<u>freecampgrounds.com</u>
<u>rv-camping.org</u>
<u>rvparkreviews.com</u>
<u>allstays.com/c/camping-free.htm</u> (look on the sidebar, Boondocking and Stops)

Membership site, Harvest Hosts, wineries and farms offering free overnight boondocking
harvesthosts.com

Membership site, network of other RVers hosting boondockers on their property
boondockerswelcome.com

There's more out there, these are just a few, so get online, and start searching "free camping", "boondocking" "blacktop boondocking", and "dry camping".

For Those Taking the Journey Out of Town

Maybe you want to make a run for it, and bug out from the big cities. You may have heard that you can **_camp for free on BLM land_**. This is true, and not quite true... some BLM campgrounds do charge, but are much cheaper (and less developed, meaning no dump sites, electricity or water) than National Parks. They are also first come, first serve, do it yourself, no reservation affairs, unlike National Parks where reservations are required. You simply find a spot, and if it is a fee area, put some money in an envelope, and drop it in a box. Also, most of the BLM land is west of the Rockies, and away from the cities. You can check **BLM.gov**, or better yet, web search "blm camping" + your state, to get areas where you can camp.

There are some free and low cost camping options you may not have heard of, such as the **Army Corps of Engineers.** The Corps has had a hand in building many dams, and at the adjacent lakes, there are campgrounds. 422 lakes in 43 states, in fact. *Web search "****Corps Lake Gateway****".*
corpslakes.usace.army.mil/visitors/camping.cfm

Also, **electric companies often have campgrounds** at the lakes associated with their hydroelectric dams. For instance, *PG&E in California has nine campsite areas across the state.*
pge.com/about/environment/pge/recreation Check your local utility companies to see if they offer recreation areas at their hydroelectric dams.

If you are a veteran, many outposts of the VFW (Veterans of Foreign Wars) will allow you to park overnight in the parking lot. *Also, there are military campgrounds available for active duty and retired military.*
militarycampgrounds.us and
freecampgrounds.com/military.html

Of course, there are state and national parks, as well as county parks. These are fee site areas, and you generally need to make reservations, especially at the most popular ones. Generally, state and county parks operate on the "put some bills in an envelope, and drop it in a box" method, or may have a ranger station at the gate to collect fees. Check your local area for state and county parks. National parks, though, generally require a credit card, and a somewhat elaborate reservation making process, through *recreation.gov*

Another thing, many small towns across the West and mid-West offer free city park camping to RVers. These are the "near ghost towns", and they may offer free parking, just to attract a little business locally, such as when you gas up, or restock on groceries. Once again, **a good, online resource for some free camping areas across the country is the** *"8 in 1 eBook" found on gypsyjournalrv.com* You may have to hunt a little for the link, it keeps moving around, but *"The 7 in 1 eBook" covers Free Campgrounds, such as these small town parks.*

Another good resource is a membership to Passport America passportamerica.com For less than $50 a year, this will get you a card that will get you 50% off campground fees, and a big catalog of participating campgrounds across the country. It could pay for itself on just one stop!

The RV Electrical System

Since we are primarily talking about working online from an RV, let's talk about the RV electrical system, since you will need electric to run your computer. The RV electrical system is really two electrical systems; an AC system, and a DC system. AC is "alternating current", and it is what you have in a regular house. DC is "direct current", and that is what you have in your car. These systems are separate in your RV. The overhead lights, the water pump, and the heater will run off your DC system, and the batteries in your RV. The wall outlets, the air conditioner, and the microwave are AC only, and will not work unless you are plugged into "shore power", meaning, plugged into an outside electrical outlet. There will be separate fuses for each; the DC fuses will be car fuses. See what type/size of fuses your RV has, and keep a few extra handy. Your RV will also have "cigarette lighter plugs" that go to the DC (battery) system. You can use these to power up your laptop and other appliances through the use of a *power inverter*. You can get power inverters at auto supply stores, and also online, such as on **Amazon**. Don't try to plug more than a 400 watt inverter into your cigarette lighter plug, it was not designed for that. If you need a more powerful inverter, then you can attach it directly to the battery, or better yet, once install .

Solar Panels

Solar panels are relatively affordable; you can have a basic 200 watt solar panel and a charge controller to keep your batteries charged, professionally installed typically for $800-$1000. If you can do it yourself, it will cost less. You can get **everything you need to install solar yourself on Amazon**. If you are doing it yourself, typically, the wires are fed through the refrigerator vent, and then to the electrical system and battery. A solar panel is an investment you will not regret! Get at least 175 watts, and many fulltime Rvers have 300+ watts on the roof. You can install a **whole house inverter**, and to power up the wall sockets, but be warned, the air conditioner won't work without massive solar and battery power, and the refrigerator will be best run on DC or propane.

A lot of people think the **portable solar panels** are the way to go, because they are affordable, and can be aimed at the sun. That is true, but you may not be able to set them up while parked at Walmart or a truck stop, or if you are in an area where you may be concerned with theft. The best plan may be, to put 175w-200w on the roof, and carry a **100w suitcase panel** for a boost when you need it.

Some typical *estimated* electrical useage of common appliances is:

Blender/food processor: 300-400 watts
portable vacuum cleaner: 500-600 watts
mini-fridge: 600 watts62
video game system: 20-30 watts
13" color TV: 80 watts
19" color TV: 160 watts
25" color TV: 225 watts
stereo amplifier: 240 watts
laptop computer: 100 watts
inkjet printer: 40 watts
fax machine: 120 watts
14" color computer monitor: 125 watts
electric heaters and blow dryers: 1,000 watts

The standard overhead lights in an RV are typically 12 volt car headlight bulbs; using your overhead lights carelessly can also drain your batteries. Replacing your incandescent bulbs with **LED lights** can save a lot of energy, typically, LEDs use 1/5 to 1/10 of the energy. (Keep in mind, LED bulbs can be expensive! You can start by just replacing the lights you use the most). You can also supplement your lighting with **solar powered lanterns**, which you can leave on your dashboard to charge during the day. You can also get **small solar chargers** for cellphones and small electronics, which you can also leave on the dashboard.

As you can see, if you are boondocking and on DC power only, there are some appliances you will simply not be able to use, and even using lights at night can kill your batteries. *You must conserve your battery power! Unless you have solar panels or a gas or diesel generator, you batteries will drain, until you plug back into shore power to recharge them.* Even if you have solar panels, if you exceed the rate of recharge, your batteries will drain. So, you must conserve your battery power, in the same way you conserve water.

If You Have a Built in Generator

If you have a motorhome with a built in generator, this will also recharge your batteries when you run it. It's advised to run your generator once a month or so, just to keep it in shape. Also, this is a small engine, and needs to have oil changes, as well as filter changes. Look up the model of your generator, and find out how often to do this, as well as the type of oil it needs. Also, you may need to plug your shore power cord into the generator, for it to power your AC system; look inside the compartment where your power cord is stored, and see if it has an outlet.

I hope you have found this starter guide to the "digital nomad" lifestyle useful! Now it's up to you, to make it happen! Best wishes of freedom and success!

www.ingramcontent.com/pod-product-compliance
Lightning Source LLC
Chambersburg PA
CBHW070353190526
45169CB00003B/1010